NATIONAL
GEOGRAPHIC
KiDS

# weird but true! 4

# 350 OUTRAGEOUS FACTS

NATIONAL GEOGRAPHIC
WASHINGTON, D.C.

4

# Some jellyfish glow.

# THERE'S A MUSHROOM NAMED AFTER SPONGEBOB SQUAREPANTS.

Deep-fried **Kool-Aid** is sold as a snack at a county fair in California, U.S.A.

**LEMONS** **CAN** **POWER** **LIGHTBULBS.**

A man skipped a rock on water **51** times in one throw.

The last thing Elvis ate was ice cream and cookies.

MILLIONS OF YEARS AGO, **THERE WAS A BIRD** IN AUSTRALIA THAT WEIGHED AS MUCH AS A **POLAR BEAR.**

More earthquakes occur in Alaska than in any other U.S. state.

Fire trucks were originally painted

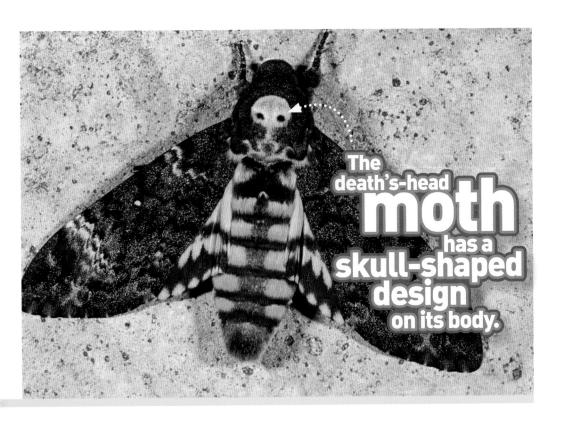

The death's-head **moth** has a **skull-shaped design** on its body.

red because that was the cheapest color.

Teams of **soccer-playing robots** compete every year at the **RoboCup.**

**MUSICIANS** PERFORMED A HIGH-FREQUENCY **ROCK CONCERT** IN AUSTRALIA THAT **ONLY DOGS COULD HEAR.**

A HORSE NEVER BREATHES THROUGH ITS MOUTH, EXCEPT IN EMERGENCIES.

# Ants
## AS BIG AS
## THIS TOY CAR
### ONCE MARCHED ON EARTH.

Hummingbird **nests** are about the size of a **golf ball.**

Laid end to end, all of the **iPhones** and **iPads** SOLd in one year would STRETCH around the **Earth.**

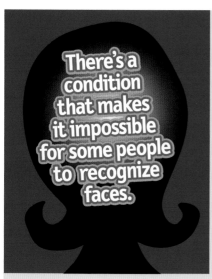

There's a condition that makes it impossible for some people to recognize faces.

The **average strawberry has 200 seeds.**

**No red M&M's** were produced between **1976 and 1987.**

**BOX** JELLYFISH HAVE EYES BUT NO **BRAIN.**

ANTARCTICA HAS **24** HOURS OF DAYLIGHT FOR PART OF THE **SUMMER.**

SOME LOBSTERS ARE ELECTRIC BLUE.

Your hands have

26 percent of the bones
in your body.

There are 27 bones
in each hand,

including your wrist.

17

Competitors race tricked-out **portable potties** at the annual **outhouse races** in Nevada, U.S.A.

# TERMITES EVOLVED FROM COCKROACHES.

GIRLS SEND AND RECEIVE MORE THAN TWICE AS MANY TEXT MESSAGES AS BOYS.

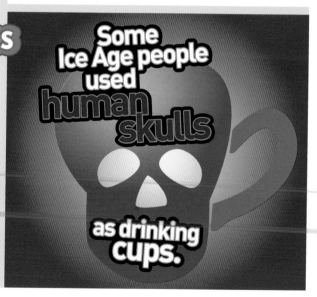

Some Ice Age people used **human skulls** as drinking **cups.**

Russian supermarkets carry **caviar-flavored** potato chips.

The **moon** can look red during a **lunar eclipse.**

The first stop signs were black and white.

The Frisbee was originally named the **Pluto Platter.**

IF A SPACE SHUTTLE COULD TRAVEL TO THE SUN IT WOULD TAKE ABOUT 220 DAYS TO GET THERE.

THERE'S AN ANNUAL

**REDHEAD FESTIVAL IN THE NETHERLANDS.**

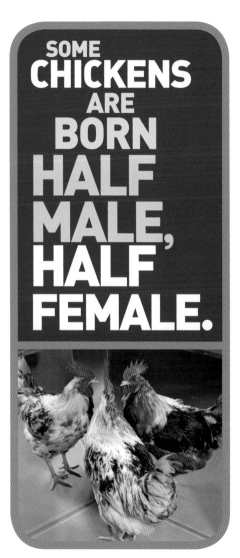

SOME **CHICKENS** ARE **BORN HALF MALE, HALF FEMALE.**

THAT'S
WEIRD!

A
**group**
of
**owls**
is called a
*parliament.*

Some **bats'** hearing is strong enough to detect the sound of a beetle walking on a leaf.

Some cave-dwelling **salamanders** don't have **eyes.**

PREHISTORIC HUMANS **CHEWED** TREE RESIN AS CHEWING GUM.

THE LONGEST NONSTOP FLIGHT BY A BIRD IS **200** DAYS.

# A pair of ruby slippers from *The Wizard of Oz* sold for more than $660,000.

# THE UNIVERSE IS FLAT.

More than **5 billion** green **Monopoly houses** have been manufactured since the **game** was introduced in 1935.

A white stork in Germany mysteriously turned blue.

There are about **three pounds** (1.4 kg) of bacteria living in your stomach.

BEES CAN SEE ULTRAVIOLET, YELLOW, BLUE, AND BLUE-GREEN, BUT NOT RED.

Each year about
# 1,000,000,000,00

# 000,000,000,000

snow crystals drop from the sky.

# Some gorillas play tag.

TAG, YOU'RE IT!

It's possible for a *seed* to blow across the ocean and *sprout* on another continent.

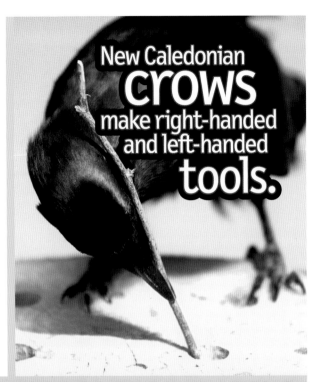

New Caledonian **crows** make right-handed and left-handed **tools.**

**Coughing while you get a shot can make it hurt less.**

MOST BATS CAN'T TAKE FLIGHT FROM THE GROUND.

A dog named **Yoda** won the World's Ugliest Dog Contest.

# A BEAVER
## COULD SWIM 16 LAPS
### IN AN OLYMPIC-SIZE POOL
## WITHOUT TAKING A BREATH.

CRABS
ARE DISTANT RELATIVES
OF SPIDERS.

LAS VEGAS, *Nevada, U.S.A.,* IS THE BRIGHTEST SPOT ON EARTH.

The largest known **snowflake** was wider than a Frisbee.

A speck of **blood** contains about **5 million** red blood cells.

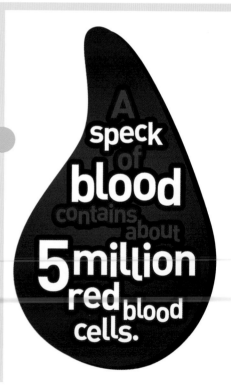

THERE'S **A WINGLESS** ANT THAT CAN GLIDE FOR **UP TO** **90** FEET.
(27 m)

can live for more than 100 years.

A FAMILY OF FIVE RODE A **FIVE-SEAT BIKE** **6,439 MILES** (10,363 km) FROM KENTUCKY TO ALASKA, U.S.A., **IN ONE YEAR.** ▶

COMPETITORS HURL THEIR OLD **CELL PHONES** FOR SPORT AT FINLAND'S **MOBILE PHONE THROWING CHAMPIONSHIPS.**

A National Geographic Channel team used **300** helium **balloons** to lift a lightweight house— with people inside!— **more than two miles into the air.** (3.5 km)

INSPIRED BY THE MOVIE UP

# AN OCTOPUS HAS RECTANGULAR PUPILS.

When there's thunder during a snowstorm, it's called

# THUNDER-SNOW.

# Odontophobia
## is the fear of teeth.

**U.S. DOLLARS ARE MADE OF COTTON AND LINEN, NOT PAPER.**

You can beat **brain freeze** by pressing your tongue to the roof of your **mouth.**

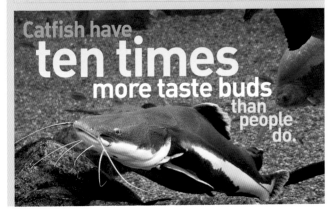

Catfish have **ten times** more taste buds than people do.

SCIENTISTS DESIGNED A ROBOTIC "EEL" THAT DETECTS POLLUTION IN WATER.

A New York, U.S.A., company INVENTED A HELMET that lets kids riding piggyback "STEER" their parents.

JUNE 30 IS ASTEROID DAY.

The lower the sun is in the sky, the higher the rainbow.

IN BASEBALL, the phrase "HITTING A CAN OF CORN" refers to CATCHING A ROUTINE FLY BALL.

A REPAIRMAN trapped in a cash machine was rescued by sending notes to customers along with their receipts.

SHORT-TAILED WEASELS PERFORM ELABORATE DANCES to mesmerize rabbits.

There's a **FULL-SCALE REPLICA** of the **GREEK PARTHENON** in NASHVILLE, TENNESSEE, U.S.A.

Old English sheepdog + poodle = **sheepadoodle**

**That's Weird!**

SCIENTISTS HAVE CREATED **A LASER** THAT'S **ONE BILLION TIMES BRIGHTER THAN OUR SUN.**

A **RACOON** in FLORIDA, U.S.A., broke into a PARKED CAR **TO GIVE BIRTH.**

## PENGUIN DROPPINGS CAN BE pink.

YOU **GROW** FASTER IN **THE SUMMER** THAN YOU DO IN THE **FALL.**

There's a fruit named "stinking" toe.

Elephants can swim for up to 6 hours without resting.

Some **sunspots**—magnetic fields on the sun—are bigger than **Earth**.

OUNCE FOR OUNCE, SOME **CATERPILLAR MEAT** CONTAINS **MORE PROTEIN** THAN LEAN BEEF.

A **150-METER** (164-yard) **pool** atop a **55-story hotel** IN SINGAPORE is the **world's** LARGEST OUTDOOR **swimming pool** AT THAT HEIGHT.

Cockleshells are heart-shaped.

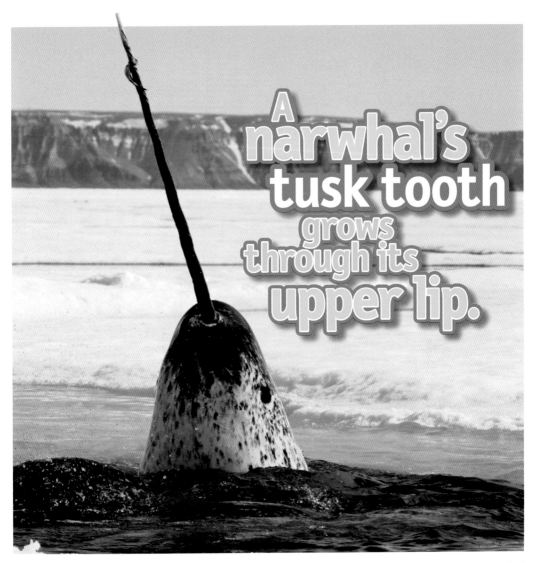

A **narwhal's** **tusk tooth** grows through its **upper lip.**

**Ripe bananas glow blue under a black light.**

# A **MONTH** ON VENUS IS LONGER THAN A **DECADE** ON VENUS.

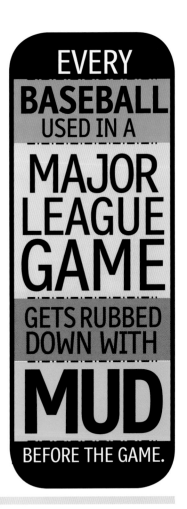

EVERY **BASEBALL** USED IN A **MAJOR LEAGUE GAME** GETS RUBBED DOWN WITH **MUD** BEFORE THE GAME.

**Bats' knees face** backward.

IT TAKES THOUSANDS OF YEARS FOR LIGHT TO TRAVEL FROM THE SUN'S CORE TO ITS SURFACE.

If you could **drive to the sun,** it would take about **190 years** to get there.

The **moon** weighs
81,000,000,000,000,000,000 tons.
(73,000,000,000,000,000,000 t)

WATERMELONS
ARE
**92%**
WATER.

-40°F  -40°C

**-40°** is the only temperature that is the same in Celsius and Fahrenheit.

# A WOODPECKER
CAN PECK A TREE
UP TO 30 TIMES A SECOND.

*Ostrich plumes were once worth twice their weight in gold in London, England.*

A bridge built in Lima, Peru, is reportedly held together by **egg whites.**

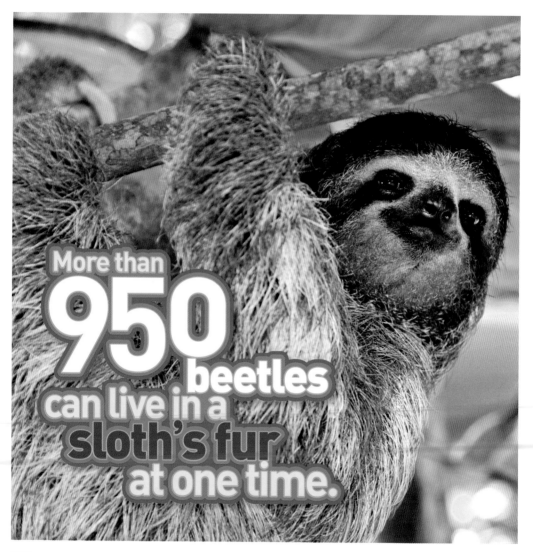

More than **950** beetles can live in a sloth's fur at one time.

You are **rarely** more than **six feet** (1.8 m) away from a **spider.**

THE WORLD'S MOST STOLEN FOOD is CHEESE.

YOUR SKIN SHEDS AND REGROWS ONCE A MONTH.

An astronaut once lost a **SPATULA** during a space walk.

# THE EIFFEL TOWER GETS
## REPAINTED EVERY SEVEN YEARS.

A man wrote an entire **novel** without using the letter **"e."**

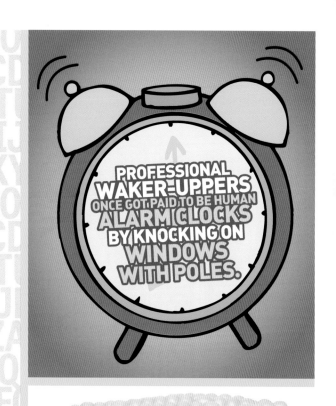

PROFESSIONAL WAKER-UPPERS ONCE GOT PAID TO BE HUMAN ALARM CLOCKS BY KNOCKING ON WINDOWS WITH POLES.

There is almost always an **even number of rows** on an ear of corn.

Many astronauts **crave** Tabasco sauce in space.

PIRANHAS BARK.

Sound travels 15 times faster through steel than through air.

SOME SPIDERS SPIN WEBS

Some musicians with amnesia can still remember how to play music.

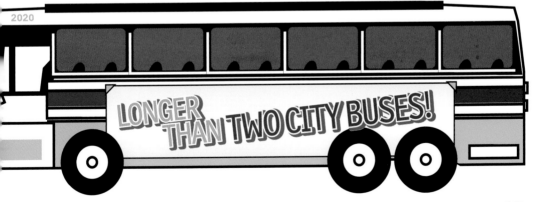

LONGER THAN TWO CITY BUSES!

# A GROUP OF
# TURKEYS

TOADS DO NOT HAVE TEETH.

**THE SPATULA-TAILED HUMMINGBIRD'S TAIL IS SO HEAVY THAT IT CAN ONLY FLY FOR A FEW SECONDS.**

ONE OF JUPITER'S MOONS, CALLED EUROPA, MAY HAVE TWICE AS MUCH WATER AS ALL THE OCEANS ON EARTH.

# SOME MAMMAL SPECIES GROW BIGGER IN COLD CLIMATES.

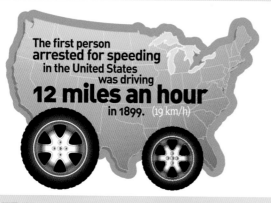

The first person arrested for speeding in the United States was driving **12 miles an hour** in 1899. (19 km/h)

A kangaroo **rat** does not need to **drink water.**

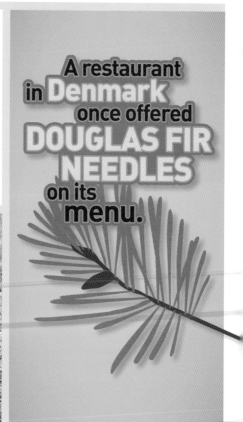

A restaurant in **Denmark** once offered **DOUGLAS FIR NEEDLES** on its **menu.**

THERE'S **ENOUGH PAINT** ON THE **WORLD'S LARGEST** *PASSENGER JET* **TO COVER TEN** BASKETBALL COURTS.

71

There is a **trap** designed to catch **Bigfoot** in a **forest** in Oregon, U.S.A.

# THE WORLD'S FASTEST TYPIST CAN REACH SPEEDS OF 200 WORDS PER MINUTE.

**Porcupine quills were once used as toothpicks.**

A puppy in California, U.S.A., was so tiny it was smaller than an iPhone!

AT TWO WEEKS OLD

THE ENERGY IN
ONE BOLT OF
LIGHTNING
COULD TOAST ABOUT
100,000
SLICES OF BREAD.

**AFGHANISTAN** AND **AZERBAIJAN** ARE THE ONLY COUNTRIES THAT BEGIN, BUT DON'T END, WITH THE **LETTER A.**

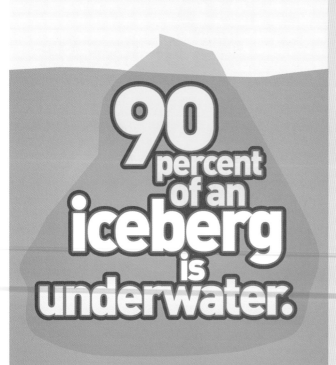

**90** percent of an **iceberg** is **underwater.**

A TEENAGER CREATED A **STAPLE CHAIN** THAT'S AS LONG AS A CRUISE SHIP.

There are more than twice as many chickens on Earth as people.

Moviemakers invented a new language for the made-up **Na'vi people** in the movie *Avatar*.

# Šnail slime can be used to soften skin.

Some **wasps** use pebbles as hammers to build their nests.

STOMACH ACID CAN DISSOLVE METAL.

NASCAR DRIVERS CAN LOSE 5 TO 10 (2.3 to 4.5 kg) POUNDS IN SWEAT DURING ONE RACE.

There's a
beach in the
Bahamas where you
can swim
with wild pigs.

# Eleven
## miles an hour
is the (17.7 km/h)
# fastest
## a vehicle
has ever
driven on the
# moon—
that's about as fast
as you ride a bike!

## CANADA'S
POSTAL CODE
FOR THE
**NORTH POLE** IS
# HOH OHO.

Santa Claus
North Pole
Hoh Oho
Canada

# SOME PREHISTORIC PEOPLE
# USED MAMMOTH BONES
# TO BUILD THEIR HOMES.

People in the **MIDDLE AGES** thought that **water in rivers** flowed from the **CENTER OF EARTH.**

**A MAN** in California, U.S.A., **ROBBED A CELL PHONE** store **WEARING SOCKS** on his **HANDS.**

**PEANUT BUTTER** CAN **MOISTURIZE HAIR.**

**A FIVE-FOOT** (1.5-M) **GIANT SHIPWORM** THAT LIVES NEAR UNDERSEA HYDROTHERMAL VENTS **"EATS" CHEMICALS.**

The **SLOWEST SUNSETS** happen around the **SUMMER AND WINTER SOLSTICES.**

**NEW YORK CITY'S BROOKLYN BRIDGE** has **14,060** miles (22,627 km) of wire— that's longer than twice the distance from London to Hong Kong.

In French text lingo, **"LOL"** is **"MDR,"** for *mort de rire,* which means **"DYING OF LAUGHTER."**

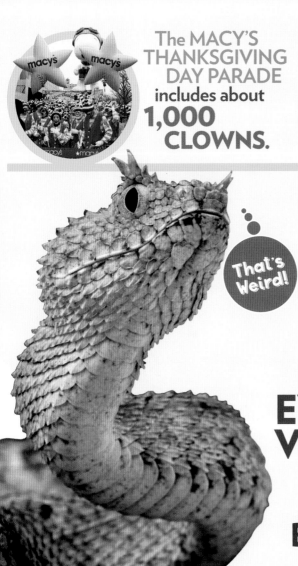

The MACY'S THANKSGIVING DAY PARADE includes about **1,000 CLOWNS.**

**A BRITISH ARTIST** created a **26-foot** (8-m)-tall sculpture out of **FOUR TONS** (3.6 t) of **RECYCLED COMPUTER PARTS.**

That's Weird!

A man from Punjab, India, set a **NEW WORLD RECORD** by spinning a **BASKETBALL ON TOP OF A TOOTHBRUSH** he held in his mouth FOR NEARLY A MINUTE.

**A CENTIPEDE** discovered in **SOUTHEAST ASIA CAN RUN UNDERWATER.**

**EYELASH VIPER EGGS** hatch inside their **MOTHER'S BODY.**

A
giant
anteater
is
6 feet
long, (1.8 m)
yet its
mouth
is as small
as a grape.

# FUNGUS CAN GROW OUT OF A ZOMBIE ANT'S HEAD.

EWW, FUNGUS!

One gold coin sold for a whopping $7.4 million.

In Japan, the "OK" sign means "Pay me."

IT TAKES A **WET DOG** LESS THAN A **SECOND** TO SHAKE OFF **HALF** OF THE **WATER** ON ITS FUR.

PORTIONS OF **ALBERT EINSTEIN'S BRAIN** ARE ON DISPLAY IN A MUSEUM IN PHILADELPHIA, PENNSYLVANIA, U.S.A.

**Tasmanian devils** sometimes **sneeze** to challenge other devils to a fight.

A FASHION **DESIGNER** CREATED A NEW **FABRIC** MADE ENTIRELY FROM **MILK.**

**Silly Putty** was used aboard **Apollo 8** to keep tools **from floating** around the ship.

TOOTHPASTE WAS ONCE MADE FROM CUTTLEFISH BONES.

THE FASTEST A PERSON HAS EVER SOLVED A RUBIK'S CUBE IS 4.73 SECONDS; A ROBOT DID IT MORE THAN FOUR SECONDS FASTER.

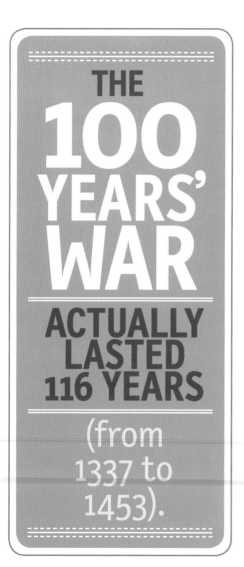

THE **100 YEARS' WAR** ACTUALLY LASTED 116 YEARS (from 1337 to 1453).

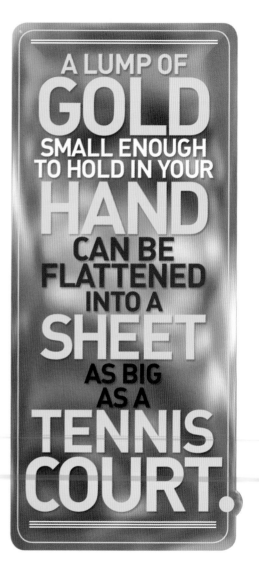

A LUMP OF **GOLD** SMALL ENOUGH TO HOLD IN YOUR **HAND** CAN BE FLATTENED INTO A **SHEET** AS BIG AS A **TENNIS COURT.**

An elephant's **tooth** can weigh as much as a **bowling ball.**

During the rainy season, **the water spilling over Africa's Victoria Falls** could fill **1,635 Olympic-size swimming pools in one hour.**

# THE WORLD'S LONGEST BEAVER DAM

## IS ABOUT AS LONG AS 60 SCHOOL BUSES LINED UP END TO END.

The average **cherry tree** produces enough **fruit** every year to fill **28 pies.**

DUCT TAPE HAS BEEN USED TO REMOVE A WART.

DON'T TRY THIS AT HOME!

Butt🔘ns were once made from mussel shells.

THE BRAIN DOESN'T FEEL PAIN.

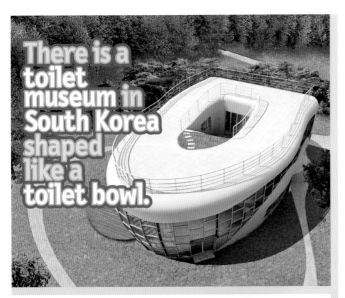

There is a toilet museum in South Korea shaped like a toilet bowl.

CROCODILES SWALLOW ROCKS TO HELP DIGEST THEIR FOOD.

PEOPLE IN **SCOTLAND** USED TO CURE **BUTTER** BY **BURYING** IT IN **PEAT BOGS** FOR **SEVEN YEARS.**

MILLIONS OF YEARS AGO, **AUSTRALIA'S DESERTS** WERE AS WET AND LUSH AS A RAIN FOREST.

*It can take up to three weeks to make a* **Jelly Belly** *jelly bean.*

**Surgeons sometimes use sea coral to replace human bone.**

A STUDY FOUND THAT **DAIRY COWS** MAY PRODUCE MORE **MILK** WHILE LISTENING TO **CLASSICAL MUSIC.**

107

TWO TEENAGERS **LAUNCHED** A LEGO MAN **85,000 FEET** (25,900 m) INTO **SPACE** USING A **HOMEMADE WEATHER BALLOON.**

A **mouse** can squeeze through a **hole** the **size** of a piece of popcorn.

ASTRONAUT ALAN SHEPARD HIT **GOLF BALLS WHILE ON THE MOON.**

**DOLPHINS EVOLVED FROM EARLY ANCESTORS OF GIRAFFES AND CAMELS.**

PEOPLE IN THE UNITED STATES **EAT MORE BANANAS** THAN **APPLES** AND ORANGES COMBINED.

**AN ARTIST CREATED A ONE-TON, LIFE-SIZE MAMMOTH OUT OF RECYCLED FARM EQUIPMENT.**

You can make paper out of dryer lint.

The Statue of Liberty's **torch** sways up to **5 inches** (12.7 cm) in the wind.

Artists in Italy created a pink stuffed **rabbit** big enough to see from space!

Wearing blue-tinted sunglasses may make you less hungry.

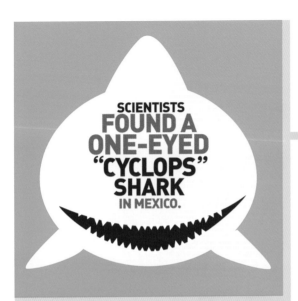

SCIENTISTS **FOUND A ONE-EYED "CYCLOPS" SHARK** IN MEXICO.

MALE MICE **SING** TO **ATTRACT** POTENTIAL **MATES.**

After recycling almost all of their waste, one family of four was able to fit a year's worth of trash in a spaghetti sauce jar.

Most household **dust** contains dead skin.

Pumice
is the
only rock
that can
float in water.

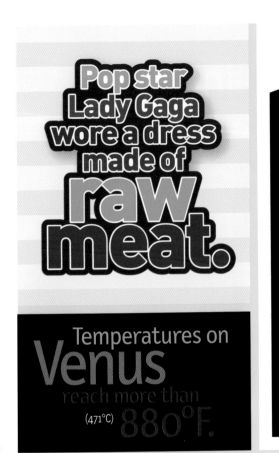

Pop star Lady Gaga wore a dress made of **raw meat.**

Temperatures on **Venus** reach more than (471°C) **880°F.**

A **RAT** CAN **SURVIVE** A **FALL** FROM A FIVE-STORY BUILDING.

YOU MAY MAKE BETTER DECISIONS **WITH A FULL BLADDER.**

A
7-foot-9-inch
(2.1-m)
basketball
player
can
dunk
without
jumping.

THE RAINIEST PLACE
IN THE CONTINENTAL UNITED STATES
—ABERDEEN, WASHINGTON—
GETS **11 FEET**
**OF RAIN** (3.4 m)
EVERY YEAR.
IF IT FELL ALL AT ONCE,
THE WATER WOULD BE ABOUT
4 FEET (1.2 m) HIGHER THAN A BASKETBALL HOOP.

**LILY PADS** CAN GROW TO BE **WIDER THAN** A KING-SIZE **BED.**

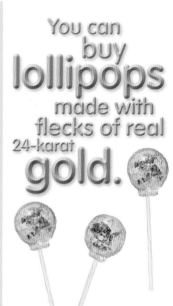

You can buy **lollipops** made with flecks of real 24-karat **gold.**

THE WORLD'S HEAVIEST INSECT, THE **giant weta,** IS BIG ENOUGH TO **EAT A CARROT.**

WHEN A KID LOSES A **TOOTH** IN GREECE, **HE THROWS IT ON THE ROOF!**

THE WORLD'S **RICHEST MAN** IS WORTH MORE THAN **$85 billion—** that's enough to buy a fleet of a million sports cars.

Every 50 years, rocks from Mars fall to Earth.

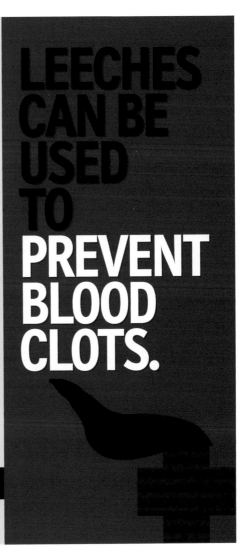

LEECHES CAN BE USED TO **PREVENT BLOOD CLOTS.**

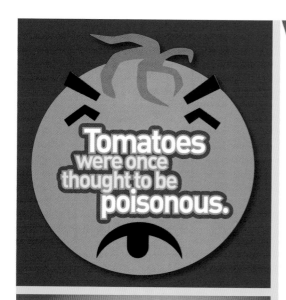

Tomatoes were once thought to be **poisonous.**

Strawberry- and chocolate-covered **Cheetos** WERE SOLD IN JAPAN.

WALKING USES 200 MUSCLES.

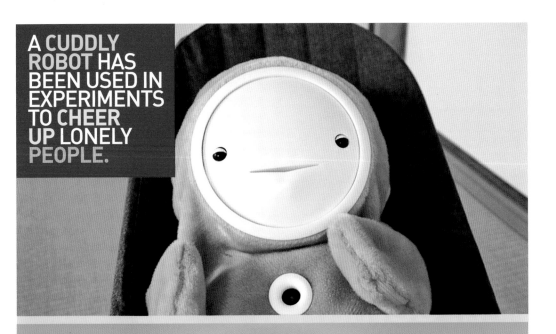

A CUDDLY ROBOT HAS BEEN USED IN EXPERIMENTS TO CHEER UP LONELY PEOPLE.

A CAR COULD DRIVE AROUND EARTH 87 TIMES ON THE AMOUNT OF FUEL IT TAKES TO FILL A JUMBO JET'S TANK.

Some
Greenland
sharks
may live to be
200
years old.

Some **JUMPING SPIDERS** will chase **LASER POINTERS.**

**THERE IS NO LOCAL TIME ZONE AT THE NORTH POLE.**

Some **GOLF SHOTS** are known as **"BANANA BALLS"** for their **CURVING PATHS.**

There's a village named **GIGGLESWICK** in **NORTH YORKSHIRE, ENGLAND.**

**Sunflowers** can **remove radioactive material** from the soil they're planted in.

AN **ICEBERG** ABOUT THE SIZE OF DELAWARE, U.S.A., **BROKE OFF ANTARCTICA** IN 2017.

Researchers found a **3,000-YEAR-OLD PROSTHETIC BIG TOE** in an **Egyptian** tomb—the oldest artificial body part found so far.

**HORSEY McHORSEFACE** IS A **THOROUGHBRED RACEHORSE** from Australia.

124

**AN APP** can notify you when **YOUR CAT ENTERS AND LEAVES** through a pet door.

The fossil of a **110-MILLION-YEAR-OLD DINOSAUR** was **DISCOVERED** by a SHOVEL OPERATOR in a Canadian mine.

Some PINEAPPLES are PINK **INSIDE**.

That's Weird!

All the concrete used in a year could create an **89-FOOT** (27-m)-**HIGH WALL** around the **EQUATOR**.

Every GIRAFFE has a unique COAT PATTERN.

**ONE OF THE WORLD'S LARGEST**

# ICEBERGS

**IS BIGGER THAN NEW YORK CITY, U.S.A.**

## "*TWITCHERS*"
### ARE PEOPLE WHO TRAVEL AROUND THE GLOBE TO SEE RARE BIRDS.

Most frogs eat their skin after they shed it.

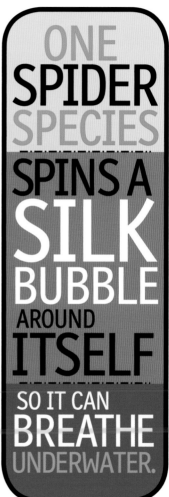

ONE **SPIDER** SPECIES SPINS A **SILK** BUBBLE AROUND **ITSELF** SO IT CAN **BREATHE** UNDERWATER.

THERE ARE NO COFFEE SHOPS IN A TOWN CALLED **HOT COFFEE,** IN MISSISSIPPI, U.S.A.

Some **tarantulas** defend themselves by shooting **itchy hairs** into the skin of their predators.

PEOPLE CAN BE ALLERGIC TO THE COLD.

The average **hug** lasts three seconds.

SOME TOADS CAN DETECT EARTHQUAKES BEFORE THEY HAPPEN.

When glass breaks, the cracks move

faster than

3,000 miles an hour. (4,800 km/h)

A **SEA OTTER** HAS A MILLION HAIRS ON **ONE SQUARE INCH** (6.5 sq cm) OF ITS BODY.

EXTRACTS FROM HUMAN HAIR ARE USED TO MAKE SOME PIZZA CRUSTS.

133

**The *Agathidium vaderi* slime-mold beetle is named after Darth Vader because of its shiny, helmet-like head.**

The **dwarf gecko,** one of the world's tiniest **lizards,** can fit on your **fingernail.**

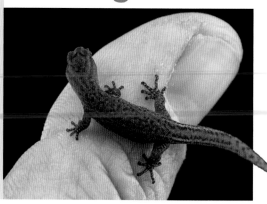

The **dot** over the letters **i** and **j** is called a **tittle.**

THERE ARE MORE
MOBILE
DEVICES
connected to the
WEB
THAN THERE ARE PEOPLE
LIVING ON EARTH.

PEANUT BUTTER WAS INVENTED AS A SOURCE OF PROTEIN FOR PEOPLE WITHOUT TEETH.

It takes **540 peanuts** to make one 12-ounce (340-g) **jar** of **peanut butter.**

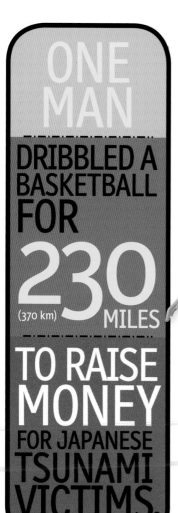

**ONE MAN** DRIBBLED A BASKETBALL FOR **230** (370 km) **MILES** TO RAISE MONEY FOR JAPANESE TSUNAMI VICTIMS.

BARBIE'S FULL NAME IS BARBARA MILLICENT ROBERTS.

A LEOPARD WITH A STRAWBERRY-COLORED COAT WAS SPOTTED IN SOUTH AFRICA.

JIGSAW PUZZLES WERE ONCE CALLED "DISSECTED MAPS."

A WALRUS **TUSK** CAN GROW TO BE AS LONG AS A **BOOGIE BOARD.**

SOME PEOPLE
HIRE GOATS
TO MOW
THEIR LAWNS.

# LAKE CHARGOGGAGOGGMANCHAUGG
## IN MASSACHUSETTS, U.S.A., HAS THE

Some **cobras** can spit venom up to **6.5 feet—** (2 m) that's longer than a hockey stick!

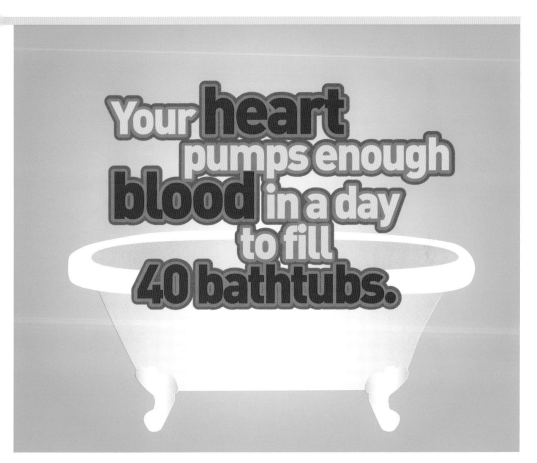

Your **heart** pumps enough **blood** in a day to fill **40 bathtubs.**

IF YOU COUNTED ALL OF THE HOURS ANGRY BIRDS **FANS** HAVE SPENT PLAYING THE GAME, IT WOULD ADD UP TO MORE THAN **ONE MILLION YEARS.**

# There is
## no land on
# Saturn.

You can buy socks made from bamboo.

# A BLACK HOLE
## CAN WEIGH AS MUCH AS
# 10 BILLION SUNS.

# IN MALAYSIA, PEOPLE TEXT "HA3" INSTEAD OF LOL.

## A toy car—
dipped in **gold** and covered in **diamonds** and **rubies**— sold for **$60,000** at a charity auction.

# SCIENTISTS GREW PLANTS FROM 32,000-YEAR-OLD SEEDS.

# YOUR RIGHT LUNG IS A LITTLE BIGGER THAN YOUR LEFT LUNG.

# A rainbow looks different to every person who sees it.

YOU WILL LIKELY GET MORE THAN 600 COLDS IN YOUR LIFETIME.

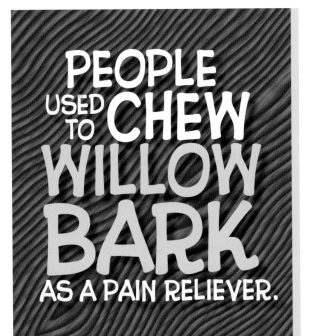

PEOPLE USED TO CHEW WILLOW BARK AS A PAIN RELIEVER.

Spider silk has been used to make violin strings.

56 MILLION YEARS AGO, HORSES WERE THE SIZE OF HOUSE CATS.

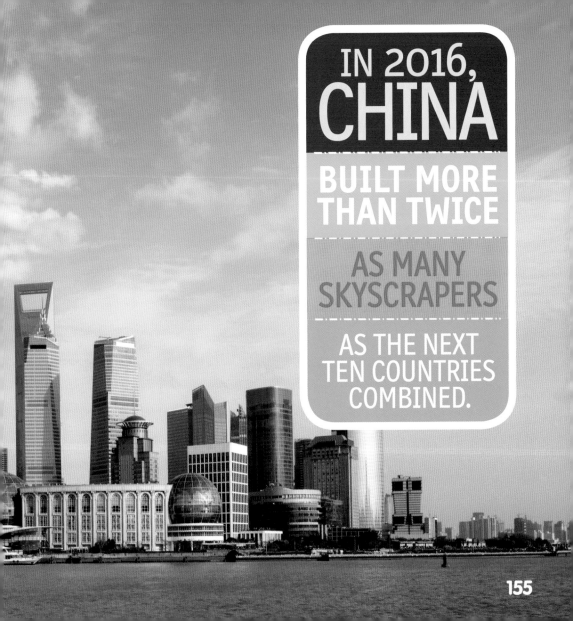

IN 2016,
CHINA

BUILT MORE
THAN TWICE

AS MANY
SKYSCRAPERS

AS THE NEXT
TEN COUNTRIES
COMBINED.

It's possible to **snow ski** on the Big Island of Hawaii.

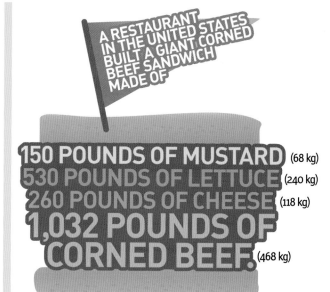

A RESTAURANT IN THE UNITED STATES BUILT A GIANT CORNED BEEF SANDWICH MADE OF

**150 POUNDS OF MUSTARD** (68 kg)
530 POUNDS OF LETTUCE (240 kg)
260 POUNDS OF CHEESE (118 kg)
**1,032 POUNDS OF CORNED BEEF.** (468 kg)

THE AVERAGE TEENAGER KNOWS ABOUT 60,000 WORDS.

THE TALLEST KNOWN
# DINOSAUR,
## *SAUROPOSEIDON PROTELES,*
WAS TALLER THAN A
SIX-STORY BUILDING.

**A giraffe sleeps 1½ hours a day.**

THE FASTEST **robot** WITH LEGS COULD OUTRUN AN ELEPHANT

THERE ARE OVER
A BILLION
MOTOR VEHICLES
ON THE PLANET.

There are more than 700 versions of the story of Cinderella.

**A GROUP OF MUSICIANS** IN CHINA MAKES **INSTRUMENTS** OUT OF SWEET POTATOES, CARROTS, AND OTHER **VEGETABLES.**

A *BLUE WHALE'S LARGEST VEINS* **ARE SO BIG** *YOU COULD SWIM THROUGH THEM.*

.There is a ski-up Starbucks at a ski resort IN THE UNITED STATES.

A GROUP OF **GREEN** anacondas **IS CALLED** A **BED.**

In 2007, A MAN SWAM **THE ENTIRE LENGTH** of the AMAZON RIVER— longer than the distance from **NEW YORK CITY TO LOS ANGELES— IN 66** DAYS.

A FERRIS WHEEL in SHANGHAI, CHINA, is located on the ROOF of a SHOPPING MALL.

**A STRAY DOG** walked onstage and **SAT** by a **VIOLINIST** during an **ORCHESTRA CONCERT** in Ephesus, Turkey.

The mechanical **SHARKS** used in the 1975 movie **JAWS** were named **BRUCE.**

Some artists use **AVOCADO PITS AND FLESH** to create **ELABORATE ART.**

There is a **CHEMICAL ELEMENT** named after the STATE OF CALIFORNIA.

THE STRATOLAUNCH—**THE LARGEST AIRPLANE IN THE WORLD**—HAS A WINGSPAN LONGER THAN AN AMERICAN FOOTBALL FIELD.

BRITISH PRIME MINISTER **WINSTON CHURCHILL** WAS AN ACCOMPLISHED **ARTIST**.

SATURN'S MOON **ATLAS** looks like a FLYING SAUCER.

**A NINE-YEAR-OLD BOY** found a **1.2-MILLION-YEAR-OLD FOSSIL** by tripping over it.

*That's Weird!* •••

SCIENTISTS HAVE CREATED A **PATCH WITH 100 MINIATURE NEEDLES** THAT DISSOLVE INTO THE SKIN TO **DELIVER A FLU VACCINE**.

IN NEW ENGLAND, U.S.A., A **"JAKE"** IS AN **AFFECTIONATE TERM FOR A FIREFIGHTER**.

# MAIL IS STILL DELIVERED BY MULE TO THE REMOTE TOWN OF SUPAI, ARIZONA, U.S.A.

**SOMEONE TRIED TO SELL A CHICKEN McNUGGET SHAPED LIKE GEORGE WASHINGTON'S HEAD ON eBAY FOR $8,100.**

CHICKENS WITH WHITE EARLOBES LAY WHITE EGGS; CHICKENS WITH RED EARLOBES LAY BROWN EGGS.

One **ostrich egg** is equal to **two dozen** chicken eggs.

ABOUT
**ONE IN A THOUSAND EGGS**
HAS A DOUBLE YOLK.

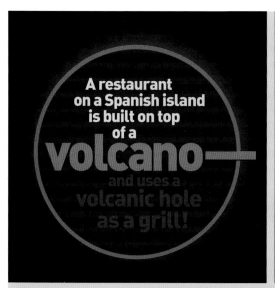

A restaurant on a Spanish island is built on top of a **volcano**—and uses a volcanic hole as a grill!

The Atlas **moth** has a **wingspan** as wide as a **toaster.**

SOME FRUIT DRINKS GET THEIR **PINK COLOR** FROM THE **EXTRACT OF COCHINEAL BUGS.**

THE LEAVES OF A CERTAIN **PALM TREE** CAN GROW TO BE AS LONG AS TWO STRETCH LIMOS.

A CAT USES **TINY HOOKS** ON ITS **TONGUE** LIKE A **HAIRBRUSH** DURING GROOMING.

171

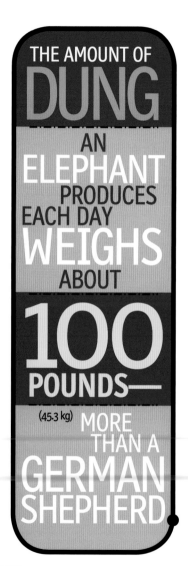

THE AMOUNT OF **DUNG** AN **ELEPHANT** PRODUCES EACH DAY **WEIGHS** ABOUT **100** **POUNDS—** (45.3 kg) MORE THAN A **GERMAN SHEPHERD.**

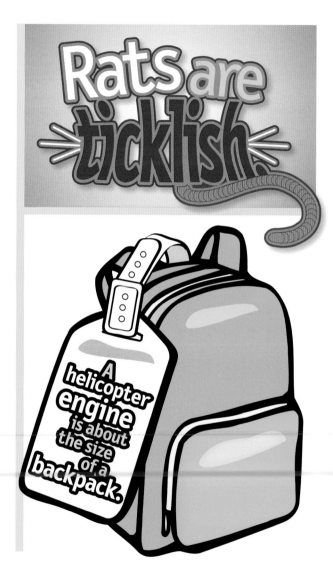

Rats are ticklish.

A helicopter engine is about the size of a backpack.

AN EXCITED **GUINEA PIG** JUMPS STRAIGHT UP.

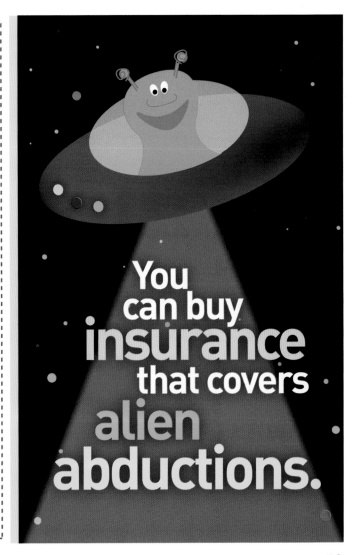

You can buy **insurance** that covers alien abductions.

THE
SCARLET
IBIS
GETS ITS COLOR FROM THE
RED
CRABS
IT EATS.

175

One in **1,000** people can't smell a **skunk's** spray.

THAT'S WEIRD!

SOME **PEOPLE** WHO HAVE LOST A LIMB CAN STILL FEEL IT.

Moondust **smells** like burnt gunpowder.

IT TAKES **6 MINUTES** TO MAKE A MARSHMALLOW PEEP.

More people live in the Tokyo, Japan, metro area than in all of Canada.

IT TAKES ABOUT **460 GALLONS** OF WATER (1,741 L) TO MAKE **ONE** HAMBURGER.

You can buy cupcakes through 24-hour ATMs.

CLOUDS FORM LOWER IN THE SKY THAN THEY USED TO.

TREES WITH **SQUARE TRUNKS** GROW IN PANAMA.

# There's a foam replica of Stonehenge in Virginia, U.S.A.

One
out of every
**10,000**
**clovers**
is a
**four-leaf**
**clover.**

**BABIES BLINK ONLY ONCE OR TWICE EVERY MINUTE— ADULTS BLINK 10 to 15 TIMES.**

A SWISS JEWELER CREATED A RING MADE ENTIRELY OF DIAMOND—INCLUDING THE BAND!

In China you can buy green tea cream-flavored Oreo cookies.

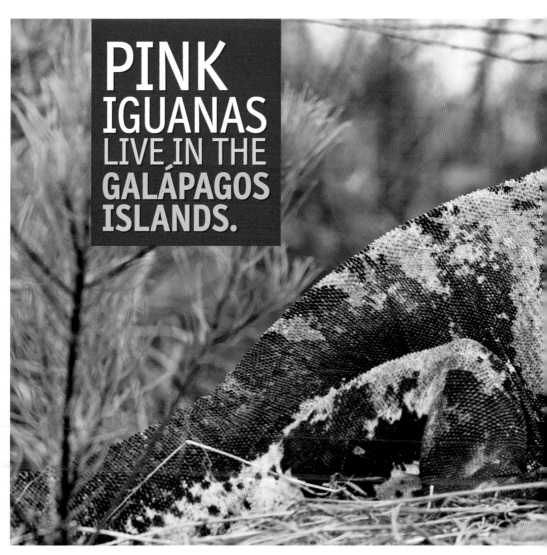

PINK
IGUANAS
LIVE IN THE
GALÁPAGOS
ISLANDS.

People who fear numbers suffer from arithmophobia.

# ISTANBUL, TURKEY, IS LOCATED ON TWO CONTINENTS:

ASIA

EUROPE

# EUROPE AND ASIA.

**A squid** can change its color and pattern in 700 milliseconds— almost in the **blink of an eye.**

The village of **Tilt Cove** in Newfoundland, Canada, has a population of

**4**

In the future, you may be able to take a **space elevator** thousands of miles above Earth.

The technical term for the pound sign on a phone is octothorpe. #

THE TEN MOST VENOMOUS SNAKES IN THE WORLD LIVE IN AUSTRALIA.

A two-pound truffle— a rare mushroom— (0.9 kg) once sold for more than $300,000.

The first bicycles didn't have pedals.

ONE IN
1,461
PEOPLE ARE
BORN ON
LEAP
DAY.

The Olympic flame travels with its own guards.

195

AS YOU TRAVEL CLOSER TO THE SPEED OF LIGHT TIME SLOWS DOWN.

A DUTCH COMPANY HAS MADE A **FLYING** THREE-WHEELED CAR THAT CAN REACH **112 miles an hour** (180 km/h) ON LAND OR IN THE AIR.

THERE ARE **NO RIVERS IN** SAUDI ARABIA.

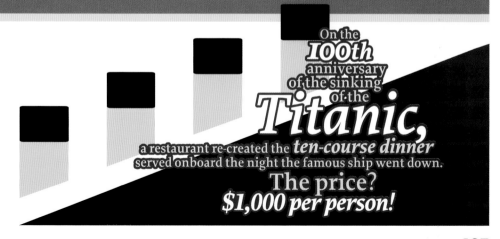

On the **100th** anniversary of the sinking of the **Titanic,** a restaurant re-created the *ten-course dinner* served onboard the night the famous ship went down. The price? *$1,000 per person!*

SCHNAUZER + POODLE

**SCHNOODLE**

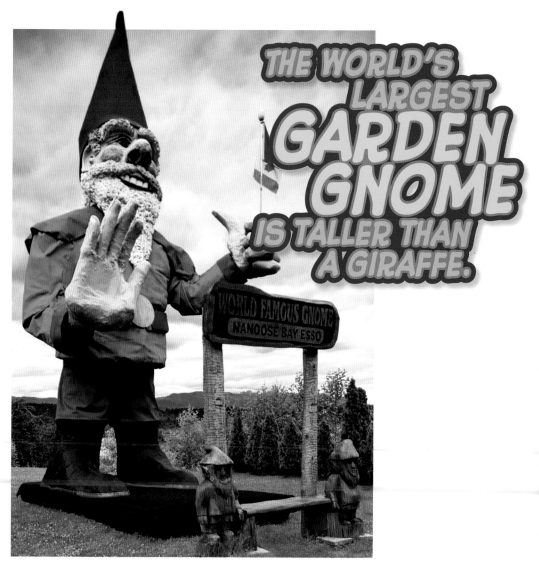

THE WORLD'S LARGEST **GARDEN GNOME** IS TALLER THAN A GIRAFFE.

WORLD FAMOUS GNOME
NANOOSE BAY ESSO

THE JACKFRUIT—THE LARGEST FRUIT THAT GROWS ON A TREE—CAN WEIGH UP TO 110 POUNDS. (50 kg) THAT'S THE WEIGHT OF 293 APPLES!

Some **artists** in Mexico paint portraits on baked **tortillas.**

**TULIP BULBS** WERE ONCE USED AS A KIND OF **CURRENCY** IN **HOLLAND.**

There's a **snail** that floats by making a **bubbly raft** out of its mucus.

YOU MAY SPEND UP TO HALF OF YOUR WAKING HOURS DAYDREAMING, ACCORDING TO ONE STUDY.

# GUESS WHAT?

Your tongue would reach down to your belly button if you were a _____!
## WHAT?

Ladybugs sometimes play pretend!
## WHEN?

## WANNA FIND OUT?

Hot water freezes faster than cold water!
## WHY?

The FUN doesn't have to end here! Find these far-out facts and more in *Weird But True! 5*.

*weird but true! 5*
350 OUTRAGEOUS FACTS

## NATIONAL GEOGRAPHIC KiDS

## AVAILABLE WHEREVER BOOKS ARE SOLD
Get a fun freebie at natgeokids.com/fun-pack

# FACTFINDER

**Boldface** indicates illustrations.

## A

*A* (letter) 76
Aberdeen, Washington, U.S.A. 117
Afghanistan 76
*Agathidium vaderi* 134
Airplanes 71, **71**, 121, 164, **164**
Alarm clocks 62, **62**
Alaska: earthquakes 8
Aliens 173, **173**
Amazon River, South America 164
Amnesia 65
*Angry Birds* (video game) 146
Antarctica 14, 124
Anteaters **86–87**, 87
Ants 12, 36, 88, **88**
Apollo 8 94
Apples 109
Apps 125
Arithmophobia 188
Asteroid Day 44
Astronauts 59, 63, **63**, 108
Atlas (moon) 165, **165**
Atlas moths 170
ATMs 44, 178, **178**
Australia
    deserts **104–105**, 105
    poisonous snakes 194
    prehistoric bird 8
    rock concert for dogs 12
*Avatar* (movie) 78, **78–79**

Avocados 164, **164**
Azerbaijan 76

## B

Babies 183, **183**
Bacteria 27
Bahamas 82, **82**
Balloons 39, **39**, 108
Bamboo **148–149**, 149
Bananas 52, **52**, 109
Barbie (doll) 138, **138**
Baseball 44, **44**, 53
Basketball 85, **85**, 116, **116–117**,
    118, 138
Bats 24, **24**, 32, 53
Beaches **54–55**, 82, **82**
Beavers 32, 100
Bees 27
Beetles 58, 134
Bicycles 37, 195
Bigfoot 72, **72–73**
Black holes 150
Black lights 52, **52**
Bladders, full 115
Blinking 183
Blood 36, 119, 145
Blue (color)
    bananas 52, **52**
    lobsters 15, **15**
    stork 27, **27**
    sunglasses 112, **112**

Blue whales 163
Body parts, artificial 124, **124**
Bones 16, **16–17**, 83, 94, 106
Box jellyfish 14
Brain 14, **14**, 91, 102
Brain freeze 43
Bridges 57, **57**, 84, **84**
Brooklyn Bridge, New York City,
    U.S.A. 84, **84**
Butter 103
Buttons 102, **102**

## C

California, U.S.A.
    deep-fried Kool-Aid 7, **7**
    element named after 164
    robber wearing socks on
        hands 84
    tiny puppy 74, **74**
Camels 109, **109**
Carrots 118, **118**, 163, **163**
Cars 45, **55**, 121, **160–161**, 197, **197**
Caterpillars 47, **47**
Catfish 43, **43**
Cats 125, **125**, **153**, 171, **171**
Cell phones 37
Centipedes 85
Chalk 38, **38**
Chargoggagoggmanchauggagog-
    gchaubunagungamaugg, Lake,
    Massachusetts, U.S.A. 144–145

**209**

# FACTFINDER

# FACTFINDER

# FACTFINDER

# PHOTOCREDITS

Published by National Geographic Partners, LLC.
All rights reserved. Reproduction of the whole
or any part of the contents without written
permission from the publisher is prohibited.

Since 1888, the National Geographic Society has
funded more than 12,000 research, exploration,
and preservation projects around the world.
The Society receives funds from National
Geographic Partners, LLC, funded in part by
your purchase. A portion of the proceeds from
this book supports this vital work. To learn
more, visit natgeo.com/info.

NATIONAL GEOGRAPHIC and Yellow Border
Design are trademarks of the National
Geographic Society, used under license.

For more information, visit
nationalgeographic.com, call 1-877-873-6846,
or write to the following address:

National Geographic Partners
1145 17th Street N.W.
Washington, D.C. 20036-4688 U.S.A.

Visit us online at nationalgeographic.com/books

For librarians and teachers:
ngchildrensbooks.org

More for kids from National Geographic:
natgeokids.com

For rights or permissions inquiries, please
contact National Geographic Books Subsidiary
Rights: bookrights@natgeo.com

Designed by Rachael Hamm Plett, Moduza Design

First edition published 2012
Reissued and updated 2018

Trade paperback: 978-1-4263-3110-7
Reinforced library binding ISBN:
978-1-4263-3111-4

The publisher would like to thank Jen Agresta,
project manager; Robin Terry, project manager;
Julie Beer, researcher; Michelle Harris,
researcher; Sarah Wassner Flynn, project
editor; Paige Towler, project editor; Eva
Absher-Schantz, art director; Julide Dengel,
art director; Kathryn Robbins, art director;
Ruthie Thompson, designer; Lori Epstein,
photo director; Hillary Leo, photo editor;
Alix Inchausti, production editor; Anne
LeongSon and Gus Tello, production assistants.

Printed in China
23/PPS/3